Bodhi Goes to China!

达摩

To the Grand Poobah and his Duseydoer, the friends and mentors who gave line to the lure.

Artist: Michael Blendermann
Illustrations: Inscribe Graphics
Printed in China

Copyright © 2013 by Tommy Tong
ISBN: Hardback – 978-1-940827-02-5
ISBN: Ebook – 978-1-940827-05-6
ISBN: Kindle – 978-1-940827-08-7

A long time ago, a monk from India decided to cross the highest mountain range in the world so he could give Buddhism to China. His name was Bodhi. He was no ordinary man and this was no ordinary journey.

1

The Himalayas divide India from China. They have many dangerous animals and are very rugged and ice capped. Still today, many people get lost or hurt while hiking in these mountains and never make it out.

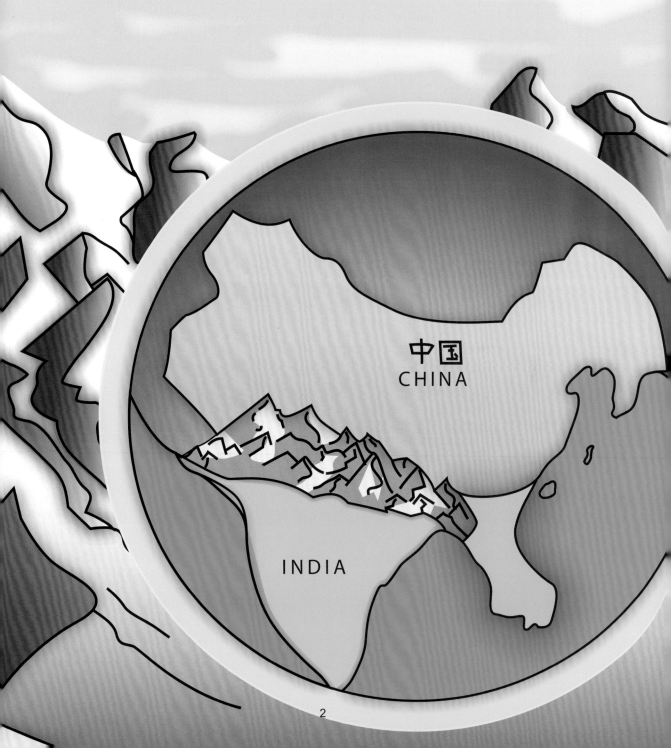

中国
CHINA

INDIA

It took Bodhi many months to cross the Himalayas in his sandals. During his journey he studied all of the animals he saw; cranes, tigers, snakes, leopards, monkeys and many more. Bodhi watched the way they hunted, attacked and defended themselves.

As Bodhi practiced the movements of the animals, his body became stronger and his mind became more alert. He felt closer to nature and stronger in spirit.

When Bodhi got to China, Emperor Wu was very happy to see him and wanted to learn all about Buddha. Bodhi taught the emperor many things but could not stay at the palace very long. He knew that he belonged in a monastery and wanted to leave.

Emperor Wu was sad to see Bodhi go but agreed to build many monasteries for monks all over China. The two men said their goodbyes and Bodhi headed off into the heart of China, a place that some believe is the heart of the world.

Bodhi travelled west to a very sacred area known as *The Five Great Mountains*. It is said that the god *Pangu* laid down to rest there after he created the world. The mountains are what remain of his body.

At the base of the center mountain is a small monastery called Shaolin. Bodhi knew that this was where he would stay, but the head monk would not let him in.

Bodhi hiked up into the mountains and found a cave where he waited patiently year after year, asking every Spring to be allowed into the monastery. For nine years, Bodhi waited in his cave meditating and practicing his animal movements.

It is said that Bodhi's shadow can still be seen on the walls of the cave today and if you enter the cave, you can feel his wisdom rushing through your soul.

One Spring, Bodhi was finally allowed to join the monastery. But when he did, he was not very happy with what he saw…

The monks in Shaolin were skinny and weak. They were often beaten up and robbed when they went to town. Most of them were not strong enough to sit for hours in meditation to train their minds.

The monks had been given a nice temple by the emperor and they tried to study all of the ancient wisdom, but they did not have a wise man to lead them. Over the years, the monks and the monastery had fallen into very bad shape.

Bodhi knew exactly what to do. He cleaned up the monastery and began teaching the monks his animal exercises that he had now been doing for nine years. These exercises were known as *The 18 Hands of Lohan*.

The exercises helped heal sick monks and make them all stronger so they could do their chores, meditate for long hours and even defend themselves. Soon the monastery became famous and people came from all over China to study at the monastery in Shaolin.

By now, Bodhi's animal movements had become a full set of exercises for the mind, body and spirit. These movements are believed to be the beginning of martial arts by students all over the world, and the Shaolin monastery its considered it's birthplace.

The Chinese call these exercises Gong Fu. Westerners often call it *Kung Fu,* but either way, it simply means effort and commitment. The monks now worked very hard in everything they did and the monastery soon grew very large.

The monks all took a vow of secrecy and would not share their martial art with anyone outside of the monastery. For hundreds of years, only Shaolin monks were able to learn Kung Fu. Still today, martial arts of all kinds like to keep many secrets.

But bad times had fallen on China long after Bodhi was gone, and the new emperors needed young men in the army, not in the monasteries. The emperors often closed the monasteries all over China and sometimes forced the monks to flee. As they fled, they continued to practice and teach their arts and beliefs.

中国
China

South East
Asia

People from all over the world began to hear of the many Shaolin monks spread out all over China practicing and teaching their ways. Many people came from other countries to find them and learn from them. As these people returned home, they took with them the movements that they liked best.

The Koreans were farmers who pulled plows all day, so they liked to use their legs for kicking. The Japanese were fishermen who pulled nets from the sea so they liked to use their arms more.

The southern countries with lots of bamboo liked to use sticks to fight. The people from the island of Okinawa were not allowed to have weapons in their country after being conquered by Japanese Samurai, so they studied all of the exercises that could be done with empty hands.

Today there are many different kinds of martial arts, but most people believe these all came from Bodhi's first studies of animal movments.

Kung Fu

Kali

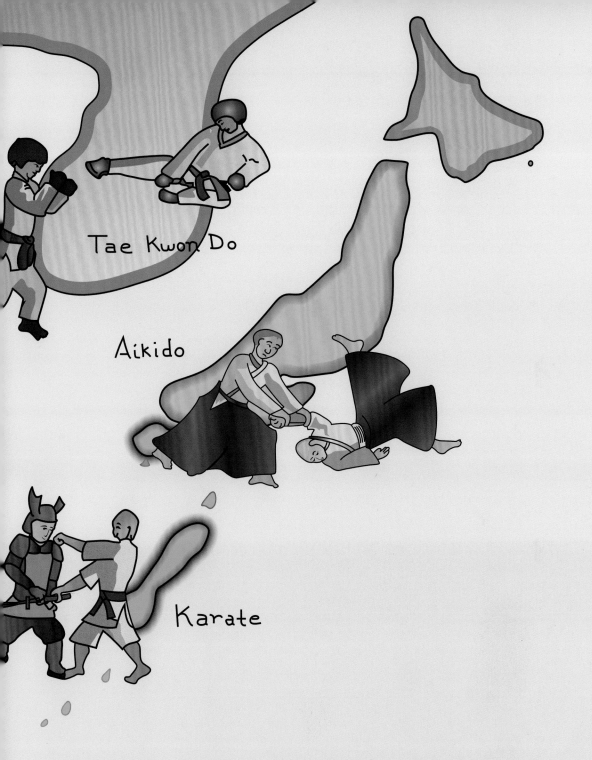

Tae Kwon Do

Aikido

Karate

In the old days, belts were used to keep baggy pants up and shirts tucked in. Over time, a student's belt would get darker with sweat and hard work. The most senior students of martial arts still wear the darkest belts for that reason today.

The Shaolin monastery has been destroyed and rebuilt many times over the years. Today it is home to thousands of students and monks. They train hard every day from morning until night from a very young age and are considered to be some of the best martial artists in the world.

If you visit the monastery, you will see many statues of Bodhi and many stories about his life there on the walls.

Bodhi
Bodhi the E

Bodhi is the father of Buddhism in China and is loved by hundreds of millions of people.

ama
ened One

He is also the father of martial arts all over the world and his teachings are studied by millions of people still today.

CHINA

Himalayas

INDIA

About the Author

Tommy has studied and taught martial arts for over 30 years. It was through his art that he came to learn of Bodhidharma and the relationship between knowledge, peace and power. It has been said that the path to happiness is paved with self-knowledge and Tommy has spent a lifetime in pursuit of that particular form of understanding.

Tommy's first visit to the Shaolin Monastery moved him so deeply that he has since returned several times. While meditating in Bodhi's cave, Tommy was overwhelmed by the power that still remains 1500 years after Bodhi's departure. Some have speculated that Bodhi was drawn to the area because of its power. Tommy was drawn there by Bodhi and considers it to be his most humbling and memorable experience.

Look for other amazing titles by Tommy Tong…

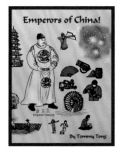